~A BINGO BOOK~

Utah
Bingo Book

COMPLETE BINGO GAME IN A BOOK

Written By Rebecca Stark

ISBN 978-0-87386-537-1

Educational Books 'n' Bingo

Printed in the U.S.A.

DIRECTIONS

INCLUDED:

List of Terms

Templates for Additional Terms and Clues

2 Clues per Term

30 Unique Bingo Cards

Markers

1. **Either cut apart the book or make copies of ALL the sheets. You might want to make an extra copy of the clue sheets to use for introduction and review. Keep the sheets in an envelope for easy reuse.**

2. Cut apart the call cards with terms and clues.

3. Pass out one bingo card per student. There are enough for a class of 30.

4. Pass out markers. You may cut apart the markers included in this book or use any other small items of your choice.

5. Decide whether or not you will require the entire card to be filled. Requiring the entire card to be filled provides a better review. However, if you have a short time to fill, you may prefer to have them do the just the border or some other format. Tell the class before you begin what is required.

6. There are 50 terms. Read the list before you begin. If there are any terms that have not been covered in class, you may want to read to the students the term and clues before you begin.

7. There is a blank space in the middle of each card. You can instruct the students to use it as a free space or you can write in answers to cover terms not included. Of course, in this case you would create your own clues. (Templates provided.)

8. Shuffle the cards and place them in a pile. Two or three clues are provided for each term. If you plan to play the game with the same group more than once, you might want to choose a different clue for each game. If not, you may choose to use more than one clue.

9. Be sure to keep the cards you have used for the present game in a separate pile. When a student calls, "Bingo," he or she will have to verify that the correct answers are on his or her card AND that the markers were placed in response to the proper questions. Pull out the cards that are on the student's card keeping them in the order they were used in the game. Read each clue as it was given and ask the student to identify the correct answer from his or her card.

10. If the student has the correct answers on the card AND has shown that they were marked in response to the *correct questions,* then that student is the winner and the game is over. If the student does not have the correct answers on the card OR he or she marked the answers in response to *the wrong questions,* then the game continues until there is a proper winner.

11. If you want to play again, reshuffle the cards and begin again.

Have fun!

TERMS INCLUDED

Agricultural

Allosaurus

Bonneville Salt Flats

Beehive

Blue Spruce

Border(s)

John Moses Browning

Bryce Canyon

Cherry (-ies)

Climate (-tic)

Coal

Colorado Plateau

Colorado River

Copper

County (-ies)

Cutthroat Trout

Dutch Oven

Elk

Executive Branch

Flag

Great Basin

Great Salt Lake

Indian Ricegrass

Judicial Branch

Kings Peak

Legislative Branch

Lowest Point

Mined

Mormon(s)

Motto

National Park(s)

Ogden

Onion(s)

Pony Express

Promontory

Rocky Mountains

Salt Lake City

Sea Gull(s)

Seal

Ski (-ing)

Song

Sundance

Topaz

Tribes

Union

Utah Territory

Wasatch Front

West Valley City

Brigham Young

Zion

Additional Terms

Choose as many additional terms as you would like and write them in the squares. Repeat each as desired.
Cut out the squares and randomly distribute them to the class.
Instruct the students to place their square on the center space of their card.

Utah Bingo

Clues for Additional Terms

Write two clues for each of your additional terms.

1. 2.	1. 2.
1. 2.	1. 2. .
1. 2.	1. 2.

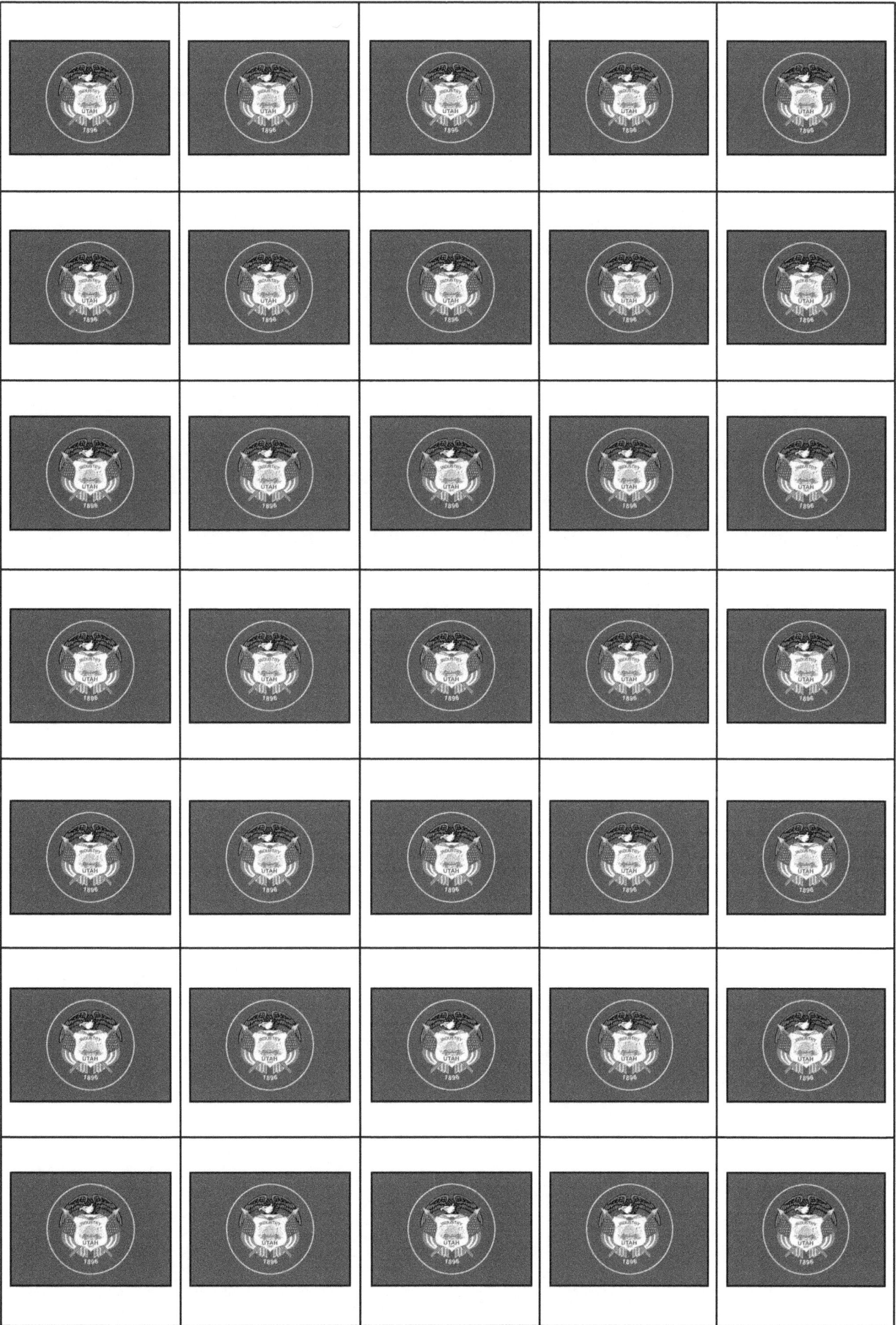

Agricultural 1. Utah's top ___ products are cattle and calves, dairy products, hogs, hay, and greenhouse and nursery products. 2. Livestock dominates the state's ___ industry. Hay, the most important crop, is grown to feed the cattle.	**Allosaurus** 1. The ___ was the predominant North American predator during the Late Jurassic. It is the state fossil. 2. Many ___ specimens have been found in two of Utah's quarries.
Beehive 1. The ___ is the official state emblem; the ___ Cluster is the official astronomical symbol; and the honeybee is the official state insect. 2. The ___ State is the official state nickname.	**Blue Spruce** 1. The ___ is the state tree. 2. The foliage of the ___ is silvery blue. This tree can withstand extremes in temperature.
Bonneville Salt Flats 1. The ___ are in the center of the Great Salt Lake Desert. 2. The ___ cover about 4,000 acres. They are named after the ancient sea that once covered the Great Basin.	**Border(s)** 1. Arizona, Colorado, Idaho, Nevada, and Wyoming ___ Utah. 2. New Mexico does not ___ Utah, but the southeastern corner of Utah touches New Mexico, Colorado and Arizona. The place where these states meet is called the Four Corners.
John Moses Browning 1. This gunsmith and inventor was born in Ogden, Utah, in 1855. 2. His inventions helped revolutionize the firearms industry in America.	**Bryce Canyon** 1. ___ in southwestern Utah comprises horseshoe-shaped amphitheaters carved from the eastern edge of the Paunsaugunt Plateau. 2. ___ is known for its geological structures called hoodoos. The red, orange, and white colors of the rocks provide spectacular views.
Cherry (-ies) 1. The ___ is the state fruit. 2. Utah is the second largest producer of tart ___ in the nation; it is the fifth largest producer of sweet ones.	**Climate (-tic)** 1. Although thought by many to be a desert state, Utah's ___ is diverse. 2. Utah has three ___ regions: humid, semi-arid, and arid. Each covers about one-third of the state.
Utah Bingo	

Coal 1. ___ is the state rock. 2. Although ___ is found in 17 of Utah's 29 counties, ___ mining is concentrated in Emery and Carbon counties.	**Colorado Plateau** 1. The ___ is the largest geographic region. It covers most of the southern and eastern Utah. Five national parks are in this region. 2. Bryce Canyon, Cedar Breaks Canyon, and Zion Canyon are all found in the ___. The region known as the Four Corners is also in the ___.
Colorado River 1. The ___ drains watersheds from 7 western states. The ___ River Basin is divided into the Upper Basin and the Lower Basin. Utah is in the Upper Basin. 2. The ___ flows southwesterly through Utah. The Green River and the San Juan River are major tributaries.	**Copper** 1. ___, the state mineral, is important to Utah's economy. 2. Most of the ___ mined in Utah comes from the Bingham Canyon mine, one of the world's largest open-pit ___ mines.
County (-ies) 1. There are 29 ___ in Utah. 2. Salt Lake ___ is by far the largest in terms of population. San Juan ___ is largest in terms of area.	**Cutthroat Trout** 1. The Bonneville ___ is the state fish. 2. The Bonneville ___ is native to Utah. Fish were very important to the Indians and the Mormon pioneers as a source of food.
Dutch Oven 1.The ___ is the official state cooking pot. 2. Logan, Utah, is the site of the World Championship ___ Cookoff. The __ was an indispensable item for the pioneers and has not changed very much today.	**Elk** 1. The Rocky Mountain ___ is the state animal. 2. Rocky Mountain ___ were once found over most of the United States, but hunters killed so many that they survive only in regions west of the Rocky Mountains, including mountain ranges in Utah.
Executive Branch 1. The ___ of state government comprises the governor, lt. governor, attorney general, state treasurer, and state auditor. 2. The governor is head of the ___ of state government. The present-day ___ is [fill in].	**Flag** 1. The Great Seal is centered on a blue field and circled by a thin gold line on the state ___. 2. The Sons and Daughters of Utah Pioneers commissioned the design of the current Utah state flag.
Utah Bingo	

Great Basin 1. The ___ is the northern part of the larger Basin and Ridge region. This extremely dry region covers the western part of Utah. 2. The Great Salt Lake Desert is in this region. The Great Salt Lake is in the northeastern corner. In Utah the ___ is called the Bonneville Basin.	**Great Salt Lake** 1. ___ is the largest natural lake west of the Mississippi River and the largest salt water lake in the western hemisphere. 2. ___ is the remnant of Lake Bonneville, an ice-age lake that covered much of the Great Basin.
Indian Ricegrass 1. ___ is the state grass. 2. In the past, ___ was used as a food staple by the Indians, especially when the corn crop failed.	**Judicial Branch** 1. The ___ interprets what our laws mean and makes decisions about the laws and those who break them. 2. There are various courts in the ___ of state government. The Supreme Court is the highest.
Kings Peak 1. At 13,528 feet above sea level, ___ is the highest point in the state. 2.___, the highest point in Utah, is found in the Uinta Range in the Rocky Mountains region.	**Legislative Branch** 1. The ___ of government comprises the Senate and the House of Representatives. 2. The ___ makes the laws.
Lowest Point 1. Beaverdam Wash is the ___ in the state. 2. The ___ in the state is 2,000 feet above sea level. Utah's mean elevation is 6,300 feet, making it the third highest state in the nation.	**Mined** 1. Petroleum and copper are the most valuable ___ products. 2. Natural gas is also an important ___ product.
Mormon(s) 1. ___ pioneers came to Salt Lake Valley seeking freedom from religious persecution. When they first came to the area, they named it "Deseret," a reference to the honeybee in *The Book of Mormon.* 2. The ___ Tabernacle Choir is an award-winning, 360-member choir.	**Motto** 1. "Industry" is the official state ___. 2. The state ___, "Industry," is associated with the state emblem, the beehive.

Utah Bingo

National Park(s) 1. Utah's ___ include Zion, Bryce Canyon, Arches, Canyonlands, Capitol Reef, and the north rim of the Grand Canyon. 2. Each year more than 2.5 million visitors come to seethe deep red cliffs and winding slot canyons of Zion ___.	**Ogden** 1. ___ Union Station is the official state railroad museum. It was a major railway hub through much of its history. 2. ___ was established by Miles Goodyear, a fur trapper, in 1846 and was originally named Fort Buenaventura.
Onion(s) 1. The Spanish Sweet ___ is the state vegetable. The sugar beet is the historical state vegetable. 2. ___ are an important cash crop. ___ farms can be found in Davis, Weber and Box Elder counties.	**Pony Express** 1. This fast mail service used mounted riders instead of traditional stagecoaches. 2. The eastern terminus of the ___ Historic Trail is located at Stagecoach Inn State Park in Fairfield. The western terminus is located at Ibapah.
Promontory 1. On May 10, 1869, the railheads of the Union Pacific and Central Pacific railroads met at ___ Summit, Utah Territory. 2. ___ is the official location of the completion of the First Transcontinental Railroad.	**Rocky Mountains** 1. The ___ in the northeast corner of the state is the smallest of the 3 geographic regions. This region comprises 2 ranges: the Uinta and the Wasatch. 2. The Uinta Range is one of the few east-west ranges in the ___. Kings Peak, the highest point in the state, is in the Uintas.
Salt Lake City 1. ___ is the capital and most populous city of Utah. 2. The Salt Lake Tabernacle is located on Temple Square in ___.	**Sea Gull(s)** 1. The California ___ is the state bird. 2. The ___ earned a reputation as protector of crops. When millions of crickets attacked the pioneers' food supplies, ___ from the Great Salt Lake came and ate most of the crickets, saving the crops.
Seal 1. At the center of the Great ___ of the state of Utah is a shield with a beehive, the word "Industry," and the date 1847. 2. American flags are on both sides of the shield on the Great ___. An American eagle is above the shield. The date of statehood, 1896, is below it. Utah Bingo	**Ski (-ing)** 1. Tourism is an important industry. Many tourists visit the state in the winter for its wonderful ___ conditions. 2. Park City is one of the many ___ resorts in Utah. © Barbara M. Peller

Song
1. "Utah, This Is the Place" is the state ___.
2. "Utah, We Love Thee" used to be the official state ___, but in 2003 it became the state hymn.

Sundance
1. The ___ Film Festival is the largest independent cinema festival in the nation.
2. The ___ Film Festival takes place every January. It is held in Park City, Salt Lake City, and Ogden, as well as at the Sundance Resort.

Topaz
1. ___ is the state gem.
2. This semiprecious gem is found in Beaver, Juab, and Tooele counties.

Tribes
1. Original inhabitants of Utah include the Bannock, the Goshute, the Navajo, the Paiute, the Shoshone, and the Ute ___.
2. There are 6 federally recognized ___ in Utah today.

Union
1. Utah was admitted into the ___ on January 4, 1896.
2. Utah became the 45th state in the ___ in 1896.

Utah Territory
1. The creation of ___ was part of the Compromise of 1850.
2. Fillmore was the capital of the ___ from 1851 to 1856. Salt Lake City was its capital from 1856 to 1896.

Wasatch Front
1. About 80% of Utah's population lives in the metropolitan region known as the ___.
2. The ___ comprises a chain of cities and towns along the Wasatch Range. Salt Lake City, Provo, and Ogden are part of this metropolitan area.

West Valley City
1. ___ is the second largest city in Utah. Four unincorporated areas merged in 1980 to form the present-day city.
2. Until 1980, ___ consisted of 4 separate communities: Hunter, Granger, Chesterfield, and Redwood.

Brigham Young
1. ___ founded Salt Lake City and was the first governor of the Utah Territory.
2. ___ was the 2nd President of The Church of Jesus Christ of Latter-day Saints. The university in Provo, Utah, is named for him.

Zion
1. ___ is not the largest national park in Utah, but it is the most visited.
2. Each year more than 2.5 million visitors come to see ___'s deep red cliffs and winding slot canyons.

Utah Bingo

Utah Bingo

Sea Gull(s)	Agricultural	Bonneville Salt Flats	Executive Branch	Blue Spruce
Dutch Oven	Allosaurus	West Valley City	Motto	Song
Wasatch Front	Mormon(s)		Promontory	Brigham Young
Utah Territory	Ski (-ing)	Union	Mined	Ogden
Pony Express	Great Salt Lake	Copper	Topaz	Kings Peak

Utah Bingo

Utah Territory	Wasatch Front	Judicial Branch	Seal	Lowest Point
Ogden	County (-ies)	Bryce Canyon	Ski (-ing)	Onion(s)
Climate (-tic)	Great Salt Lake		Indian Ricegrass	Union
Rocky Mountains	Salt Lake City	Mormon(s)	Zion	Blue Spruce
Song	West Valley City	Copper	Dutch Oven	Topaz

Utah Bingo

Great Salt Lake	Union	County (-ies)	Mined	Wasatch Front
Ogden	Allosaurus	Cherry (-ies)	Agricultural	Great Basin
Ski (-ing)	West Valley City		Onion(s)	Beehive
Mormon(s)	Climate (-tic)	Pony Express	Rocky Mountains	Judicial Branch
Topaz	Coal	Copper	Zion	Lowest Point

Utah Bingo: Card No. 3

Utah Bingo

Mormon(s)	Onion(s)	Bonneville Salt Flats	Coal	Lowest Point
National Park(s)	John Moses Browning	Agricultural	Seal	Wasatch Front
Promontory	Rocky Mountains		Kings Peak	Executive Branch
Union	Allosaurus	West Valley City	Copper	Bryce Canyon
Colorado Plateau	Song	Border(s)	Topaz	Brigham Young

Utah Bingo

Song	Blue Spruce	Ski (-ing)	Bryce Canyon	Coal
National Park(s)	Union	Cherry (-ies)	Indian Ricegrass	Allosaurus
Bonneville Salt Flats	Brigham Young		Motto	Flag
Kings Peak	Lowest Point	Sea Gull(s)	Zion	Colorado River
County (-ies)	Copper	Wasatch Front	Mormon(s)	Promontory

Utah Bingo

Beehive	Onion(s)	Judicial Branch	Lowest Point	Brigham Young
Mined	Ski (-ing)	Colorado River	Agricultural	Wasatch Front
Seal	Colorado Plateau		John Moses Browning	Indian Ricegrass
Copper	Pony Express	Zion	Border(s)	Bonneville Salt Flats
Ogden	Bryce Canyon	Sea Gull(s)	Promontory	Cutthroat Trout

Utah Bingo

Sea Gull(s)	Onion(s)	Flag	Union	County (-ies)
Ogden	Lowest Point	Great Salt Lake	Allosaurus	National Park(s)
Brigham Young	Executive Branch		Indian Ricegrass	John Moses Browning
Mormon(s)	Rocky Mountains	Cherry (-ies)	Utah Territory	Climate (-tic)
Copper	Coal	Zion	Border(s)	Beehive

Utah Bingo

Promontory	Onion(s)	Elk	Mined	John Moses Browning
National Park(s)	Bonneville Salt Flats	Seal	Brigham Young	Bryce Canyon
Cutthroat Trout	Coal		Lowest Point	Blue Spruce
Topaz	Mormon(s)	Utah Territory	Colorado Plateau	Rocky Mountains
West Valley City	Copper	Border(s)	Ski (-ing)	Ogden

Utah Bingo

Indian Ricegrass	County (-ies)	Great Salt Lake	Cutthroat Trout	Coal
Colorado Plateau	Lowest Point	Promontory	Ski (-ing)	Onion(s)
Great Basin	Sea Gull(s)		Allosaurus	Elk
Colorado River	Blue Spruce	Pony Express	Motto	Flag
Rocky Mountains	Zion	Cherry (-ies)	Utah Territory	Kings Peak

Utah Bingo: Card No. 9

Utah Bingo

Utah Territory	Mined	John Moses Browning	Seal	Cutthroat Trout
Brigham Young	Bryce Canyon	Agricultural	Allosaurus	Lowest Point
Coal	Onion(s)		Executive Branch	Climate (-tic)
Pony Express	Kings Peak	Colorado River	Zion	Great Basin
Cherry (-ies)	Ogden	Judicial Branch	Song	Promontory

Utah Bingo

Beehive	Onion(s)	Ski (-ing)	Colorado River	Ogden
Elk	Great Basin	Motto	Indian Ricegrass	Agricultural
National Park(s)	Lowest Point		Judicial Branch	Great Salt Lake
Cherry (-ies)	Wasatch Front	Zion	Coal	Utah Territory
Colorado Plateau	Copper	Sea Gull(s)	Border(s)	County (-ies)

Utah Bingo

County (-ies)	Blue Spruce	Great Basin	Mined	Indian Ricegrass
Great Salt Lake	Ogden	Bonneville Salt Flats	Border(s)	Allosaurus
Sea Gull(s)	Flag		Brigham Young	Seal
Copper	Rocky Mountains	Lowest Point	Utah Territory	National Park(s)
Onion(s)	Elk	Coal	Colorado Plateau	Bryce Canyon

Utah Bingo

Colorado River	Blue Spruce	Beehive	Great Basin	Brigham Young
Bonneville Salt Flats	Elk	Lowest Point	Indian Ricegrass	Climate (-tic)
Mined	Bryce Canyon		Great Salt Lake	Flag
Promontory	Zion	John Moses Browning	Coal	Utah Territory
Copper	Kings Peak	Border(s)	Sea Gull(s)	Motto

Utah Bingo

Dutch Oven	Lowest Point	Ski (-ing)	Indian Ricegrass	Colorado Plateau
Bryce Canyon	Sea Gull(s)	Great Basin	Allosaurus	Onion(s)
Colorado River	Executive Branch		Judicial Branch	Cherry (-ies)
Kings Peak	Zion	Coal	John Moses Browning	Beehive
Copper	Seal	Climate (-tic)	Ogden	Promontory

Utah Bingo

Motto	Indian Ricegrass	Ski (-ing)	County (-ies)	Mined
Beehive	Judicial Branch	Agricultural	Bonneville Salt Flats	Colorado Plateau
Brigham Young	Sea Gull(s)		Wasatch Front	Onion(s)
Copper	Great Basin	Elk	Zion	Colorado River
Ogden	Rocky Mountains	Border(s)	Cutthroat Trout	Great Salt Lake

Utah Bingo: Card No. 15

Utah
Bingo

Ute	County Map	Cell (map)	Indian Programs	Media
Colorado Plateau	Bonneville Salt Flats	Agricultural	Judicial Branch	Beehive
Unionist	Wasatch Front		Seagull(s)	Brigham Young
Colorado River	Zion	Elk	Great Basin	Copper
Great Salt Lake	Cutthroat Trout	Border(s)	Rocky Mountains	Ogden

Utah Bingo

John Moses Browning	Great Basin	Elk	Cutthroat Trout	Salt Lake City
Seal	Climate (-tic)	Flag	National Park(s)	Executive Branch
Colorado River	Blue Spruce		Brigham Young	Great Salt Lake
Mormon(s)	Bryce Canyon	Copper	Motto	Utah Territory
Colorado Plateau	Tribes	Border(s)	Rocky Mountains	Onion(s)

Utah Bingo

Cherry (-ies)	Sundance	Legislative Branch	Great Basin	Dutch Oven
Motto	Colorado Plateau	Zion	Executive Branch	Flag
Indian Ricegrass	Promontory		Tribes	Elk
Kings Peak	Ogden	Utah Territory	Ski (-ing)	Climate (-tic)
Pony Express	Colorado River	County (-ies)	Mined	Blue Spruce

Utah Bingo

Cutthroat Trout	Coal	Bryce Canyon	Colorado River	Seal
Onion(s)	Cherry (-ies)	Pony Express	Brigham Young	Colorado Plateau
Indian Ricegrass	Climate (-tic)		Legislative Branch	Bonneville Salt Flats
Blue Spruce	Agricultural	Zion	Utah Territory	Judicial Branch
Tribes	Great Basin	Ski (-ing)	Sundance	Beehive

Utah Bingo

Brigham Young	Beehive	Great Basin	Elk	Utah Territory
Motto	Mined	Onion(s)	County (-ies)	Executive Branch
Sundance	Coal		Allosaurus	Wasatch Front
Judicial Branch	Tribes	Pony Express	Rocky Mountains	Legislative Branch
Bonneville Salt Flats	Salt Lake City	Ogden	Promontory	Border(s)

Utah Bingo: Card No. 19

Utah Bingo

Dutch Oven	Sundance	Mined	Great Basin	Border(s)
Bryce Canyon	Great Salt Lake	National Park(s)	Pony Express	Seal
Blue Spruce	Flag		Mormon(s)	Agricultural
Song	West Valley City	Topaz	Rocky Mountains	Tribes
Union	Promontory	Salt Lake City	Utah Territory	Legislative Branch

Utah Bingo: Card No. 20

Utah Bingo

Motto	Beehive	National Park(s)	Great Basin	Song
Blue Spruce	Legislative Branch	John Moses Browning	Elk	Sea Gull(s)
Climate (-tic)	Ogden		Sundance	Ski (-ing)
Pony Express	County (-ies)	Tribes	Kings Peak	Promontory
Mormon(s)	Salt Lake City	Border(s)	Cherry (-ies)	Rocky Mountains

Utah Bingo

Cutthroat Trout	Judicial Branch	Legislative Branch	Bonneville Salt Flats	Colorado River
Seal	Mined	Wasatch Front	Elk	Allosaurus
Bryce Canyon	Executive Branch		Sea Gull(s)	Flag
Tribes	Kings Peak	Rocky Mountains	Agricultural	National Park(s)
Salt Lake City	Cherry (-ies)	Sundance	Climate (-tic)	Mormon(s)

Utah Bingo

John Moses Browning	Sundance	County (-ies)	Bonneville Salt Flats	Border(s)
Beehive	Dutch Oven	Ogden	Motto	Agricultural
Judicial Branch	Colorado River		Topaz	Sea Gull(s)
Climate (-tic)	Salt Lake City	Tribes	Cherry (-ies)	Rocky Mountains
Song	West Valley City	Promontory	Pony Express	Legislative Branch

Utah Bingo

John Moses Browning	Promontory	Dutch Oven	Sundance	Elk
Legislative Branch	Border(s)	National Park(s)	Seal	Sea Gull(s)
Flag	Cutthroat Trout		Colorado River	Climate (-tic)
Song	Topaz	Tribes	Cherry (-ies)	Blue Spruce
Union	Mormon(s)	Salt Lake City	Mined	West Valley City

Utah Bingo: Card No. 24

Utah Bingo

Mormon(s)	National Park(s)	Sundance	Ski (-ing)	Legislative Branch
Agricultural	Blue Spruce	Motto	John Moses Browning	Allosaurus
Kings Peak	Elk		Topaz	Tribes
Wasatch Front	Song	West Valley City	Salt Lake City	Executive Branch
Border(s)	Dutch Oven	Bryce Canyon	Colorado Plateau	Union

Utah Bingo

Legislative Branch	Sundance	Judicial Branch	Seal	Cutthroat Trout
Pony Express	Mined	Elk	Dutch Oven	John Moses Browning
Kings Peak	Topaz		Executive Branch	Mormon(s)
Cherry (-ies)	Bonneville Salt Flats	Song	Salt Lake City	Tribes
Flag	Colorado Plateau	Ski (-ing)	West Valley City	Union

Utah Bingo

Judicial Branch	Bryce Canyon	Sundance	Dutch Oven	Great Salt Lake
Song	Topaz	Motto	Tribes	Allosaurus
Zion	West Valley City		Salt Lake City	Mormon(s)
Cutthroat Trout	Beehive	National Park(s)	Union	Agricultural
Colorado Plateau	Executive Branch	Legislative Branch	Wasatch Front	Flag

Utah Bingo

Judicial Branch	Dutch Oven	Wasatch Front	Sundance	John Moses Browning
Great Salt Lake	Legislative Branch	Topaz	Seal	Executive Branch
West Valley City	Climate (-tic)		Flag	Pony Express
Utah Territory	Cutthroat Trout	Ogden	Salt Lake City	Tribes
Bonneville Salt Flats	Indian Ricegrass	Colorado Plateau	Union	Song

Utah Bingo

Legislative Branch	Dutch Oven	Cutthroat Trout	Motto	Indian Ricegrass
Rocky Mountains	Pony Express	National Park(s)	Flag	Wasatch Front
Kings Peak	Topaz		Allosaurus	Sundance
Great Salt Lake	Song	Lowest Point	Salt Lake City	Tribes
John Moses Browning	Elk	Union	Beehive	West Valley City

Utah Bingo

Coal	Sundance	Seal	Indian Ricegrasss	Tribes
Agricultural	Dutch Oven	Judicial Branch	Executive Branch	Allosaurus
Kings Peak	Colorado River		Flag	National Park(s)
Union	Beehive	Bonneville Salt Flats	Salt Lake City	Topaz
Song	Brigham Young	West Valley City	Legislative Branch	Wasatch Front

Utah Bingo: Card No. 30

www.ingramcontent.com/pod-product-compliance
Lightning Source LLC
LaVergne TN
LVHW061339060426
835511LV00014B/2012